Have a spooky Halloween :
what is the Halloween story? a book about the history of Halloween

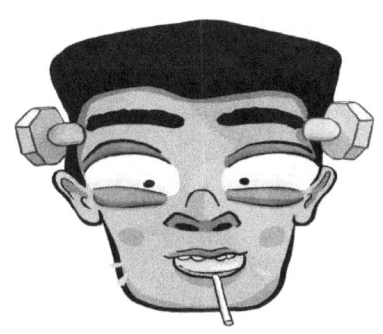

Pam Simmons

All rights reserved. No part of this publication may be reproduced, distributed, or transmitted in any form or by any means, including photocopying, recording, or other electronic or mechanical methods, without the prior written permission of the publisher, except in the case of brief quotations embodied in critical reviews and certain other noncommercial uses permitted by copyright law.

Copyright © (Pam Simons), (2022).

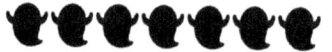

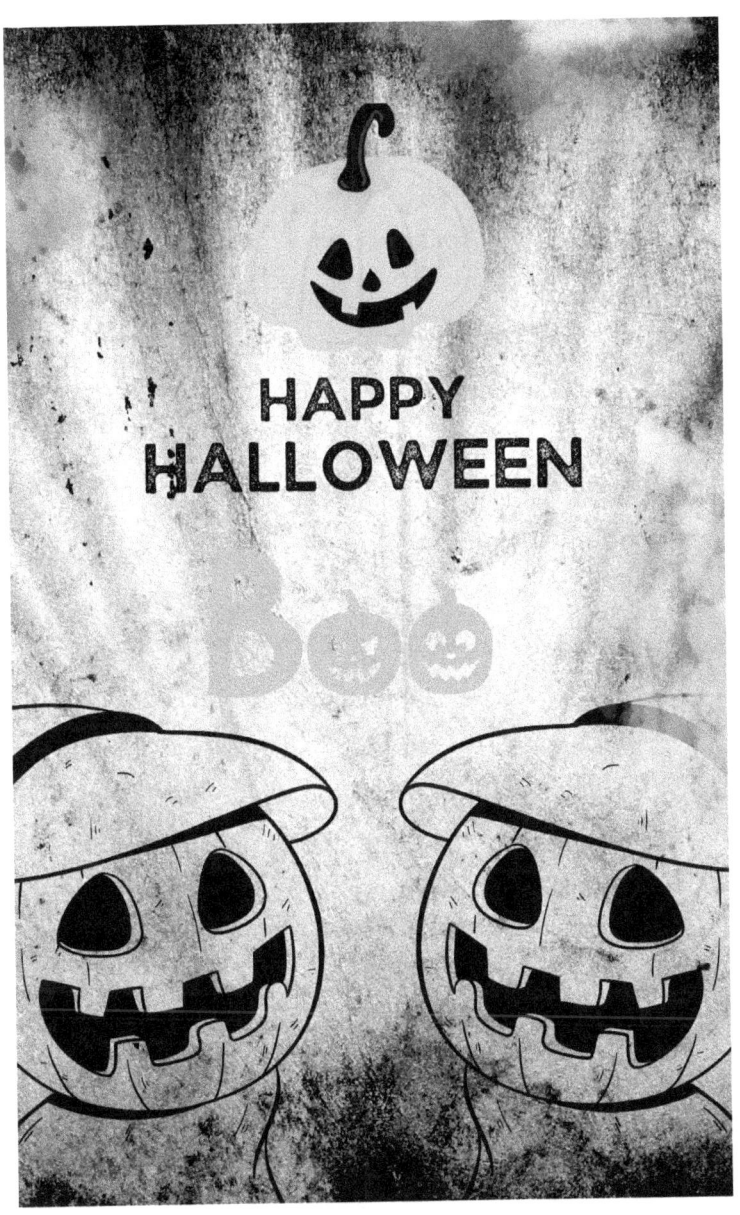

Table of contents

Chapter 1: Origins of Halloween? (All you need to know)

- Halloween's Ancient Origins
- Trick-or-Treating History

Chapter 2: Halloween games (trick or treat?)

Chapter 3 : Food and Halloween

- Halloween foods and traditions
- CANDY FOR HALLOWEEN
- A Ghostly Halloween Party
- Dia de los Muertos (Day of the Dead) [Mexico]
- The Catholic Church Relationship

Chapter 1: Origins of Halloween? (All you need to know) 🎃 👻

It was the evening before Halloween...

Okay, it's still a few nights before Halloween, but I'll take a good old haunted tale any day. America's favorite dress-up holiday is cherished by both young and old, but it has seen a lot of modifications in recent years. When communities have poor trick-or-treater attendance, the phrase "things aren't what they used to be" comes to mind.

Sure, pumpkin spice is still sprinkled on everything, and iconic Halloween flicks never grow old. Some of us have gone from trick-or-treating to trunk-or-treating in the previous two years due to social alienation. So, how much has the Halloween narrative truly evolved throughout the years? Why do

I have these wonderful Halloween activities, to begin with?

If you believe that Halloween is a distinctively American ritual, I have a trick for you! All of these favorite rituals include dressing up in a creative costume, gallivanting about in the approaching twilight to collect the finest candy from the neighbors, and meeting with friends for a monster ball. However, the autumn vacation did not begin in the United States.

In truth, the origins of Halloween can be traced back thousands of years to the Celtic festival of Samhain, which celebrated the end of the harvest season and the beginning of the new year. Samhain was also a time when the barrier between the realms of the living and the dead thinned, allowing those of us with blood still coursing through our veins to converse with loved ones who had crossed over.

Whether you believe in ghosts or not, it's always great to learn a little information before going trick-or-treating. You may discover that the holiday has a considerably more intriguing (and often much creepier!) background than you previously assumed.

Travel back in time with us to see what the earliest haunting Halloween festivities looked like, including the many ghoulies and ghosties people used to dread, what people used to carve in place of pumpkins, and even what Valentine's Day and Halloween have in common. There was no sparkly pumpkin or superhero costume to be found. If you can't get enough Halloween trivia, we've got plenty more where that came from.

Who First Celebrated Halloween?

Most experts assume that Halloween as we know it began about 2,000 years ago when Celtic people in Europe celebrated the end of the harvest and the beginning of a new year in a celebration known as Samhain (pronounced "sow-win"). According to The American Folklife Center, people also thought they could communicate with the dead more readily during that period, and they lit large bonfires to scare off ghosts.

Halloween Has a Difficult Spiritual Origin

According to History, the Celts also thought that the spiritual contact with Samhain made it easier for Celtic priests or druids to prophesy the future. They lit bonfires and sacrificed crops and animals to placate the deities. Villagers dressed up as animal heads and skins for the bonfire celebrations.

Halloween is associated with bats.

— and that, too, has historical origins. The Druids' Samhain bonfires attracted bugs, which enticed bats to come to enjoy a nice feast. Later on, numerous traditions arose mentioning bats as forerunners of death or catastrophe. A bat settling in a home, according to Nova Scotian legend, implies that a male in the family will die. If it flies about and attempts to flee, a family member will die instead.

The Romans Had Their Own Autumn Festivals

According to History, the Romans conquered most of the Celtic territory by 43 A.D. and brought their autumn festivities with them. Feralia, their October festival, also celebrated the passage of the dead. Pomona, another feast, celebrated the Roman goddess of fruit and plants. This is one of the reasons why people bob for apples during Halloween celebrations.

Christians attempted to supplant Halloween.

Fast ahead a few centuries, and the Halloween celebrations developed. Several Christian popes sought to supplant "pagan" feasts such as Samhain with ecclesiastical observances of their own. By the year 1000 A.D., All Souls' Day on November 2 had become a day for the living to pray for the souls of the dead. On November 1, All Saints' Day, also known as All Hallows' Eve, the saints were celebrated. As a result, October 31 became All Hallows Eve, which subsequently became Halloween.

The British Send Out Ghostly Gifts

Despite the new religious emphasis, the end of October was still associated with the wandering dead in Old England and Ireland. They left food offerings to appease hungry ghosts, and as time passed, humans started dressing up in scary costumes and going begging for the sweets themselves. The technique was known as "mumming," and it resembled today.

The Southern Colonies brought it to the United States.

The earliest Halloween-like celebrations in America took place in the southern colonies. People started to celebrate the harvest, share ghost tales, and even tell each other's fortunes, which were most likely a remnant of their homelands. Those early autumn festivities, however, were known as "play parties" at the time.

Women were bobbing for apples — and husbands.

In the 1700s and 1800s, women undertook Halloween rituals in the hopes of finding a spouse. Single women used to toss apple peels over their shoulders in the hopes of seeing their future husband's initials in the shapes where they landed. They also bobbed for apples during celebrations, thinking that the winner would marry first. Some people believed that standing in a dark room with a candle in front of a mirror would cause their future husband's face to show in the glass. Anyone for a Bloody Mary?

The Irish Invented Jack-o-Lanterns\shadow

The modern holiday took root in the middle of the nineteenth century, when a surge of Irish immigrants fled their homeland during the potato famine. The invaders brought with them their superstitions and rituals, notably the jack-o'-lantern. But instead of pumpkins, they carved them out of turnips, potatoes, and beets back then.

Today's Halloween is all about the treats.

By the end of the nineteenth century, more communities were engaging in a more secular (and safer) set of rituals. People began throwing Halloween parties that featured more innocuous activities, autumn seasonal delicacies, and fun costumes rather than witchcraft and nefarious mischief.

Americans spend a lot of money on candy.

Trick-or-treating gained popularity in the 1950s when Halloween became a legitimate national holiday. According to the National Retail Federation, over 179 million Americans celebrate the holiday each year, spending over $9.1 billion. That's a lot of little candy bars!

Halloween is not a recognized holiday.

Although many Americans like Halloween, it is not a federal holiday. Despite the nighttime celebrations, Halloween is still a work day, and most companies and banks operate during their usual hours. So, if you're racing home to answer your doorbell, you're not alone.

Every year on October 31, Halloween is celebrated, and Halloween 2022 will take place on Monday, October 31. The custom stems from the ancient Celtic holiday of Samhain when people would light bonfires and dress up in costumes to fend off spirits. Pope Gregory III established November 1 as a day to celebrate all saints in the ninth century.

All Saints Day soon included certain Samhain rituals. The previous evening was known as All Hallows Eve, and subsequently as Halloween. Halloween has grown into a day of activities such as trick-or-treating, carving jack-o-lanterns, celebratory parties, dressing up in costumes, and eating candy.

Halloween's Ancient Origins

The roots of Halloween may be traced back to the ancient Celtic feast of Samhain (pronounced sow-in). The Celts, who resided in what is now Ireland, the United Kingdom, and northern France 2,000 years ago, celebrated their new year on November 1.

This day signified the end of summer and the harvest, as well as the start of the dark, frigid winter, a season traditionally connected with human mortality. Celts thought that during the night before the new year, the line between the living and the dead was blurred. They celebrated Samhain on the night of October 31, when it was thought that the spirits of the dead returned to earth.

In addition to creating havoc and destroying crops, Celts believed that the presence of otherworldly spirits made it easier for

Druids or Celtic priests to prophesy the future. These forecasts were an essential source of solace throughout the long, dark winter for people who were completely reliant on the turbulent natural environment.

Druids erected massive holy bonfires to celebrate the festival when people came to burn crops and animals as offerings to the Celtic deities. During the feast, the Celts dressed up in animal heads and skins and sought to read one other's fortunes.

They re-lit their hearth fires, which had been extinguished earlier that evening, from the holy blaze to help safeguard them over the approaching winter.

The Roman Empire had seized the bulk of Celtic territory by 43 A.D. During the 400 years that they governed the Celtic kingdoms, two Roman festivals were mixed with the customary Celtic observance of Samhain.

Feralia, a day in late October when the Romans customarily celebrated the passage of the dead, was the first. The second day was dedicated to Pomona, the Roman goddess of fruits and plants. The apple is Pomona's emblem, and the inclusion of her festival into Samhain likely explains the Halloween ritual of bobbing for apples.

All Hallows' Eve

Pope Boniface IV dedicated the Pantheon in Rome to all Christian victims on May 13, 609 A.D., and the Catholic feast of All Martyrs Day was founded in the Western church. Later, Pope Gregory III enlarged the holiday to include all saints and martyrs and relocated the celebration from May 13 to November 1.

By the 9th century, Christianity's influence had extended into Celtic territories, eventually blending with and supplanting ancient Celtic traditions. The church declared November 2 All Souls' Day, a day to remember the deceased, in 1000 A.D. Today, it is commonly assumed that the church attempted to replace the Celtic celebration of the dead with a comparable, church-sanctioned event.

All Souls' Day was celebrated in the same way as Samhain was, with large bonfires, parades, and people dressed up as saints, angels, and demons. The festival of All Saints' Day was also known as All-hallows or All-hallowmas (from Middle English Alholowmesse, which means All Saints' Day), and the night before it, the customary night of Samhain in Celtic religion, became known as All-Hallows Eve and, finally, Halloween.

Halloween Has Arrived in America

Because of the strict Protestant theological systems in colonial New England, Halloween celebrations were severely constrained. In Maryland and the southern colonies, Halloween was considerably more frequent.

As the beliefs and rituals of various European ethnic groups and American Indians merged, a uniquely American form of Halloween emerged. "Play parties," which were public activities meant to celebrate the harvest, were among the earliest festivities. Neighbors would tell each other ghost tales, fortunes, and dance and sing.

Colonial Halloween celebrations also included the telling of ghost tales and other forms of mischief. Annual fall festivals were prevalent by the middle of the nineteenth century, although Halloween was not yet celebrated across the nation.

America was overwhelmed with new immigrants in the second part of the nineteenth century. These newcomers, particularly the millions of Irish escaping the Irish Potato Famine, helped to promote Halloween throughout the country.

Trick-or-Treating History

Borrowing from European customs, Americans started dressing up in costumes and going door to door asking for food or money, a practice that evolved into today's "trick-or-treat" celebration. Young ladies thought that by performing tricks with yarn, apple parings, or mirrors on Halloween, they may discern the name or look of their future spouse.

In the late 1800s, there was a movement in America to make Halloween a celebration of community and neighborly gatherings rather than ghosts, pranks, and witches. Halloween parties for both children and adults became the most popular way to commemorate the holiday around the turn of the century. Parties centered on games, seasonal delicacies, and spectacular costumes.

Newspapers and community leaders urged parents to keep anything "frightening" or "grotesque" out of Halloween festivities. By the beginning of the twentieth century, Halloween had lost much of its superstitious and religious undertones as a result of these efforts.

Halloween celebrations

By the 1920s and 1930s, Halloween had evolved into a secular yet community-centered celebration, with parades and town-wide Halloween festivities serving as the main attraction. Vandalism started to plague several festivals in many localities during this period, despite the best efforts of many schools and communities.

By the 1950s, city officials had effectively curbed damage, and Halloween had developed into a festivity aimed mostly at children. Because of the large number of small children during the baby boom of the 1950s, celebrations were shifted from local civic facilities to classrooms or homes, where they could be more readily accommodated.

The centuries-old ritual of trick-or-treating was also resurrected between 1920 and 1950. Trick-or-treating was a low-cost method for a whole town to participate in the Halloween festivities. In principle, families may also prevent pranks from being performed on them by presenting little presents to the neighborhood youngsters.

As a result, a new American custom was formed, and it has since grown. Halloween now accounts for an estimated $6 billion in yearly spending in the United States, making it the country's second greatest commercial holiday behind Christmas.

Halloween Films

When it comes to commercial success, spooky Halloween movies have a long track record. The "Halloween" series, based on the 1978 original picture directed by John Carpenter and starring Donald Pleasance, Nick Castle, Jamie Lee Curtis, and Tony Moran, is a classic Halloween film.

In the film "Halloween," a little boy called Michael Myers kills his 17-year-old sister and is imprisoned, only to escape as a teen on Halloween night and seek out his old house and a new victim. In 2018, Jamie Lee Curtis and Nick Castle starred in a direct sequel to the original "Halloween." In 2021, a sequel, "Halloween Kills," the twelfth film in the "Halloween" series overall, was released.

"Halloween," considered a classic horror film down to its eerie music, spawned subsequent renowned "slasher flicks" such as "Scream," "Nightmare on Elm Street," and "Friday the 13th." "Hocus Pocus," "The Nightmare Before Christmas," "Beetlejuice," and "It's the Great Pumpkin, Charlie Brown" are other family-friendly Halloween films.

Soul Cakes and All Souls Day

Trick-or-treating on Halloween in America is likely derived from early All Souls' Day parades in England. During the celebrations, needy residents would beg for food, and families would offer them "soul cakes" in exchange for a commitment to pray for the family's deceased relatives.

The church promoted the distribution of soul cakes as a replacement for the historical practice of leaving food and drink for wandering souls. The tradition, known as "going a-souling," was later adopted by youngsters who would visit their neighborhood households and be given ale, food, and money.

The Halloween costume has both European and Celtic origins. Winter was an unknown and dangerous period hundreds of years ago. Food supplies often ran low, and the short days of winter were fraught with anxiety for many individuals who were scared of the dark.

People expected to meet ghosts if they left their houses on Halloween when it was believed that spirits returned to the earthly realm. People would wear masks while leaving their houses after dark to avoid being identified by these ghosts, hoping that the ghosts would mistake them for fellow spirits.

To keep ghosts away from their homes on Halloween, folks would leave bowls of food at their doors to pacify the spirits and prevent them from entering.

Halloween Black Cats and Ghosts

Halloween has long been a mystery, magic, and superstition-filled festival. It started as a Celtic end-of-summer event when people felt particularly connected to dead relatives and friends. They arranged seats at the dinner table, put delicacies on doorsteps and along the side of the road, and lighted candles to assist loved ones in finding their way back to the spirit realm.

Today's Halloween ghosts are often represented as more terrifying and malicious, as are our rituals and beliefs. I try not to encounter black cats because I'm worried they'll bring us bad luck. This belief dates back to the Middle Ages when many people thought that witches escaped discovery by transforming into black cats.

I avoid walking under ladders for the same reason. This belief may have originated with the ancient Egyptians, who held triangles to be sacrosanct (it also may have something to do with the fact that walking under a leaning ladder tends to be fairly unsafe). And, particularly around Halloween, try to avoid shattering mirrors, tripping on road cracks, or spilling salt.

Halloween Matchmaking and Unusual Rituals

But what about the Halloween customs and beliefs that today's trick-or-treaters have completely forgotten? Many of these outmoded rites centered on the future rather than the past, and the living rather than the dead.

Many had to do with assisting young ladies in identifying potential spouses and promising them that they will be married someday—hopefully by next Halloween. On Halloween night in 18th-century Ireland, a matchmaking chef may conceal a ring in her mashed potatoes, believing that the diner who discovered it would find true love.

In Scotland, fortune tellers advised a young lady to name a hazelnut after each of her suitors and then hurl the nuts into the fireplace. According to legend, the nut that burnt to ashes rather than bursting or exploding symbolized the girl's future spouse. (In other versions of the narrative, the nut that burnt away represented a love that would not endure.)

According to another legend, if a young lady ate a sweet mixture of walnuts, hazelnuts, and nutmeg before going to bed on

Halloween night, she would dream of her future spouse.

Young women tossed apple peels over their shoulders, hoping for the peels to fall on the floor in the shape of their future husbands' initials; peered at egg yolks floating in a bowl of water to learn about their futures; and stood in front of mirrors in darkened rooms, holding candles and looking over their shoulders for their husbands' faces.

Other rites were more competitive. The first guest to uncover a burr on a chestnut search at certain Halloween parties would be the first to marry. Others believe that the first successful apple-bobber will be the first down the aisle.

Whether we're seeking love guidance or attempting to prevent seven years of bad luck, each of these Halloween superstitions is dependent on the kindness of the same "spirits" whose presence the early Celts felt so strongly.

Chapter 2: Halloween games (trick or treat?) 🎃

It's no wonder that October 31 is many people's favorite day of the year, with all the sweets, costumes, and frightening movies. And if you're one of those Halloween fans who go all out for the event, you're probably already haunting your home with decorations and preparing a wonderful party with family and friends. All you need now are some thrilling activities for your monster mash—and you're in luck because we've got you covered with these Halloween party games for all ages!

Timeless Halloween pastimes such as apple bobbing and corn mazes will always have a special place in our hearts. But why not up your game this year with some fresh offerings? From team challenges to smaller tournaments suited for family night, the greatest DIY Halloween game ideas for kids and adults can quickly get any scary event underway.

Most of these ideas involve just a few cheap items to produce fantastic Halloween crafts for kids, tripling the amount of quality time spent together. There are suggestions for both indoor and outdoor Halloween activities, as well as fresh spins on old favorites like tic-tac-toe, bowling, treasure hunts, ring tosses, and much more. You may also choose one that corresponds to your family's Halloween party theme.

Put on some wicked excellent Halloween music, have some Halloween treats on hand as prizes, and play these entertaining Halloween party games all night!

Halloween black light candy search

Halloween games

Halloween Candy Game with Black Lights

Play this game instead of going trick-or-treating. Your tiny ghouls and goblins may embark on a candy search using just a black lamp, scratch paper, and candy.

Trivia about Halloween
Here's some brainy entertainment! This trivia game will put your knowledge of all things spooky to the test, with questions on sweets, frightening movies, historical facts, and more.

Game 'Shoot the Skeleton'
This game will provide hours of entertainment for the kids! Simply hot glue little skeletons to a foam board and let your children aim with mini squirt guns.

Spaghetti Dig Game with Eyeballs
This one is slimy and straightforward. Put plastic eyes in a dish of cooked spaghetti noodles and watch your monsters dig them out. It's also a fantastic sensory experience!

Memory Game for Witch Hats
This exercise, which puts a witchy spin on a popular memory game, is guaranteed to get them in the Halloween mood. Hide goofy Halloween items in witch hats and see what they remember!

'I Spy' Halloween Game
I spy with my tiny eye...a fun activity that can help with the party planning! This printable "I Spy" game is easy to play and positively entertaining.

Charades for Halloween
Oh, the ghosts, mummies, and zombies! With this easy charades game, you and your children may play all of the terrifying characters.

Halloween Bingo Printable
All you have to do for this game is print and play for some friendly rivalry!

Identify the Spider on the Web
It's like Pin the Tail on the Donkey, but for Halloween! To play, just put on a blindfold and attempt to pin the adorable creepy crawlies onto their web.

Game of Fizzing Eyeballs
With this bizarre exercise, they may unleash their inner crazy scientist. The response of the bubbling vinegar when it strikes the baking soda eyes will delight both children and adults!

Hunt for Halloween Eggs
Hello there, Halloween mashup. Change the Easter baskets for cauldrons and trick-or-treat bags, and send the kids out to find Halloween-themed eggs. Of course, stuff them all full of goodies!

Crossword Puzzle for Halloween
Print out a few sheets of this Halloween crossword puzzle for your kids to work on

before going trick-or-treating. At the site below, you'll also discover a whole downloadable Halloween activity bundle for hours of fun.

Halloween Game Don't Eat Pete
This gigantic version of Don't Consume Pete will have your kids laughing—and thrilled to eat sweets!

Cornhole for Halloween
Even eight-legged creepy crawlies can enjoy this cute DIY cornhole game. It's tabletop-sized, so it's also suitable for smaller children.

Scavenger Hunt for Halloween
Halloween is the ideal occasion for a scavenger hunt! Set up clues throughout the home and watch the youngsters having a great time finding them. For added enjoyment, add a gift at the end, such as Halloween stickers.

Tossing Pumpkins for Halloween
Handmade pumpkins and even felt pumpkin bean bags are used in this DIY game. It's a Halloween game for people of all ages!

Halloween Word Search
There are never enough Halloween word games! Include this printable word scramble on your list of Halloween activities to do this year.

Ring Toss in the Dark
It turns out that duct tape can be used for almost everything. Wrap some glow-in-the-dark duct tape over glass bottles, bend some light sticks into rings, and you've got yourself a "dead" night game.

The Mummy Sack Race
Wrap white crepe paper streamers around competitors' legs to transform a sack race into a mummy sack race. That's a Halloween game right on the mummy's face!

Sensory Halloween Bags
These sensory packs are ideal for preschoolers and may be filled with Halloween-themed items such as ghostly, dreadful shaving cream with googly eyes. Just be careful to glue the bags shut before starting the games.

Return the Skeleton to its Original Position
To construct this adorable Halloween game, all you need is a little time, energy, and a few things like magnetic paint, foam board, and magnets.

Tossing a pumpkin
Tossing sugar pumpkins into these charming little cauldrons will be fun for kids.

Bowling for Mummies
Wrap a plastic set of bowling pins in toilet paper and top each with a pair of googly eyes to make a clever Halloween game.

Tic-Tac-Toe with Pumpkins
The setup for this traditional Halloween game couldn't be simpler. Simply tape a grid to a table and use one color of pumpkins for the X's and another for the O's.

Dinner Party for a Murder Mystery
It takes some preparation to make this celebration kid-friendly, but it's not difficult. (Alternatively, make it terrifying and it'll be a party your adult pals will "die" to attend.)

Stomping in the Pumpkin Patch
Kids will enjoy stomping on the balloons to get to the treasures within, such as money or wrapped bubble gum. Add a paper leaf on top of the "pumpkins" to make them more festive.

Mummy should be wrapped
To begin, divide the youngsters into two or more groups and choose one kid from each group to be the "mummy." The youngsters

may then wrap the mummy in a toilet paper roll. The squad that finishes their roll first wins!

Bowling with Pumpkins and Ghosts
This entertaining game requires just a pumpkin, toilet paper, and a black permanent marker. Remove the stem from the pumpkin to make it easier to roll.

Race the Skeleton Bones
This game, which is suitable for both teenagers and younger children, demands quick, agile fingers and just a ball of yarn and a skeleton bone.

Toss food to the Monster.
You'll have nearly as much fun DIYing this throwing game as the kids will "feeding" the monster with a feather boa on the ingredients list.

Chapter 3 : Food and Halloween

Food has long been associated with the dead in rituals that span many cultures. These began as pagan rituals and were later incorporated into the Catholic religion [All Saints Day/All Hallows Eve/All Souls Day].

Recipes and rituals adapted to local culture and cuisine. The dead in Ancient Egypt were buried with honey cakes to eat in the afterlife. At funerals in the Netherlands, mourners consumed "Does Koeks." Irish Samhain served as the inspiration for American Halloween. Sicilians honor their ancestors with cartocci and tatu. Dia de Los Muertos is celebrated in Mexico with food-laden altars for departed dining.

A common multicultural tradition is to honor the deceased with food.

The origins of Halloween and the Day of the Dead can be traced back to the Christian commemoration of the dead on All Saints' and All Souls' Day. The Celtic feast of Samhain is essential to Halloween's pagan origins... Commentators often stress the Day of the Dead's pre-Columbian beginnings in the cults of the dead that flourished among the Nahuatl-speaking peoples of central Mexico.

Hugo Nutini, an anthropologist, has...noted certain instances, such as during Tepeihuital festivals, when pictures of the deceased were put on family altars and food was presented to them, in the fashion of ofrendas so central to the Day of the Dead. Other scholars have emphasized the unusual gastronomic features of the Aztec burial ceremony, in which wooden statues of the deity Huitzilopochtli, the sun deity who arose every dawn from the soil goddess Coatlicue, were coated with an amaranth seed dough that was then consumed by the celebrants.

Halloween foods and traditions

Halloween as we know it now is a highly contemporary take on an old pagan tradition. The key connecting themes are autumn cuisine, mumming, and divination. According to our research of old cookbooks and newspapers, Americans started celebrating Halloween in the early twentieth century. Themed parties were popular at the time. As the century advanced, so did the number of party ideas for adults, teenagers, and children. Trick-or-Treat, as we know it today, did not begin until after World War II.

Halloween...is supposed to have evolved from the Celtic peoples' pre-Christian holiday known as Samhain...

Samhain was the main feast day of the year, which started on November 1st. As part of the festivity, bonfires were traditionally lit. During Samhain, it was thought that the ghosts of individuals who had died in the preceding twelve months were permitted passage to the otherworld... Scholars know very little about the genuine Samhain practices and beliefs.

The majority of accounts were not written down until centuries after Ireland was converted to Christianity...and then by Christian monks documenting old sagas.

According to the evidence, Samhain was a key point of the seasonal cycle, and traditions of laying out food and drink offerings to console the traveling spirits had joined the bonfire ritual.

Also, the ritual of mumming—dressing up and performing from house to house in return for food or drink, as well as pranking, possibly a typical activity of the wandering spirits, or just a customary pastime widespread across Europe—had become a component of the celebration... Halloween was introduced to North America by Irish and British colonists, although it was not extensively celebrated until the nineteenth century due to a massive inflow of European immigrants.

Traditional Halloween cuisine and customs: Samhain, Ireland This ancient winter holiday is typically observed on November 1, which is the Feast of All Saints in the Christian calendar. Halloween is the feast's vigil, a night when charms and incantations were potent, people gazed into the future, and feasting and revelry were ordered.

Until recently, this was a day of abstinence, when no flesh meat was permitted by church decree. The celebratory meal included colcannon, apple cake, and barm brack, as well as apples and nuts. Colcannon was made in a frying pot with a big circular bottom, three small legs, and two ear-like handles on the sides, and it was made with mashed potatoes, chopped kale or green cabbage, and onions... Champ, an Armagh term for mashed potatoes, sweet milk, and chopped chives or onions, was another favorite, eaten like colcannon by dipping each mouthful into the well of butter.

It was also customary to make champ when the first of the fresh potatoes were unearthed. Another Halloween favorite was boxty pancakes.

Grated raw potatoes were wrung in a cloth, sieved, and combined with baking powder, salt, and an egg that had been properly beaten. A sufficient amount of sweet milk was added to create a pancake batter. These were served hot, buttered, and dusted with caster sugar. They may also be turned into farls and cooked on a griddle... Apple potato cake, also known as fadge in the northeast of the nation, was a popular meal prepared using a potato cake mixture of freshly cooked potatoes, a little salt, melted butter, and flour to bind.

The mixture was split in half and rolled into circles. Layers of sliced apples were put on the bottom of the fadge, followed by the pastry cover. It was placed in a pot-oven on a bed of red-hot turf to cook. When the fadge was about done, the sides were cut, the top was flipped back, and the apples were lavishly coated with brown sugar and a big knob of butter.

The fadge was then returned to the oven to melt the sugar and butter into a sauce. A ring was placed in the cake, and it was predicted that whoever received the ring would marry by the end of the year. Cattle might be carried in or sheltered in the byres, and all potatoes and oats should be dug and piled by Halloween. It was thought that puca spits on blackberries and apples during the night following Samhain, thus they should not be harvested. The devil shook his club and shook his blanket at these fruits, according to legend in the Glens of Antrim.

The traditional ritual of placing food out for the fairies on Halloween was still practiced in portions of north Leinster and Ulster. On Halloween and All Souls' Night, 2 November, a plate of champ, complete with a spoon, was placed at the foot of the closest fairy thorn (hawthorn or whitethorn) or the gate entry to a field. Some saw it as a ceremony for the deceased, while others saw it as a sacrifice to the fairies.

The connection between food and fairies is strong, especially in the festivals, the majority of which date back to pre-Christian times. On Halloween, an informant in Layde, Co Antrim, recalls her grandmother making thick oatcakes with a hold in the center. A cord was connected through the hole, and each youngster that entered was wearing an oaten cake around her neck... This historic event is still observed not just in the United Kingdom, but also across the New England states of America.

Children in town and country continue the age-old tradition of dressing up in masks and costumes and traveling from house to home gathering apples and nuts for the Halloween celebration...

Following the traditional colcannon meal, young people performed games such as ducking for apples in a barrel or basin of water or letting the peel of an apple fall on the ground in the hope that it would reveal the first letter of a sweetheart's name.

Courting couples enjoyed sitting around the fire exchanging tales and roasting nuts...

Almost all of the games and rituals that night were about love and courtship: the ring buried in the colcannon or barmbrack symbolizing marriage, or, more sadly, the thimble denoting spinsterhood. Many sections of the nation placed the first and final spoonfuls of colcannon into the girl's stocking, which was then hung from a nail in the door in the hope that her future husband would be the first to enter.

Another ritual was for a female to walk into the night blindfolded to pluck a head of cabbage.

The size and form of the root represented her future spouse's size and shape... Another tradition was to chop nine yarrow stems with a black-handled knife. Part of the enchantment required the girl not to talk from the time she started eating her colcannon until the whole family had gone to bed... Another charm required a female to eat an apple in front of a mirror at midnight while brushing her hair. As the clock struck twelve, her prospective husband would peer over her right shoulder.

The most wonderful feast of the year was usually the Halloween meal at home. Amhlaoibh O'Suilleabhain wrote in his journal on October 31, 1831, "A lovely dry, overcast day." I had a lovely night eating apples, burning nuts, sipping tea, and eating apple pie.

Halloween meals in the United States

Halloween is maybe the only American holiday not tied with a specific feast or cuisine. Irish immigrants brought the October 31 festival to the United States in the nineteenth century. On that night, it was customary to distribute soul cakes to guests in exchange for commitments to pray on behalf of deceased relatives.

They also hang vegetable lanterns in the windows to welcome ghosts and wandering spirits...

Carved pumpkin jack-o'-lanterns are an important feature of Halloween celebrations, yet they are seldom eaten...

Pies are made using smaller species of cheese pumpkin, pie pumpkin, or sweet pumpkin, which have sweeter, less watery flesh...

Some people dry, roast, and salt the seeds as a snack...

American harvest festivities are known as play parties before contemporary Halloween.

Snap Apple Night or Nut Crack Night celebrations were held in various parts of the United States in the mid-nineteenth century and included activities such as dunking for apples...

In the late nineteenth century, middle-class Americans rediscovered (and remade)

Halloween practices to make them acceptable. Articles about Halloween began to emerge in magazines in the 1870s, encouraging a new, more consistently celebrated Victorian celebration.

Halloween parties for both children and adults had grown popular by the twentieth century...

Candies shaped like corn kernels and pumpkins were developed to mark the harvest season. In the 1880s, the Wunderle Candy Company of Philadelphia was the first to commercially create candy corn.

There are several tales about the origins of the Halloween Jack-o-lantern. The Irish claim it first, telling the story of Jack, a miserly man who once fooled the Devil into transforming himself into a sixpence, then snapped the money into his pocket and made the Devil swear not to come after him for a year. When the Devil came back for

Jack after another stingy and nasty year, Jack fooled him into climbing up a tree to select a huge, gorgeous apple from a high branch.

Jack swiftly cut the sign of the cross in the tree's trunk, preventing the Devil from climbing down, and made him swear not to come after Jack for ten years. When Jack died, he traveled to Heaven, but Saint Peter refused him entry due to his stingy attitude. Jack attempted Hell but was astonished to discover that the Devil refused to allow him to enter. The Devil had to uphold his word, and he wasn't fond of Jack.

As a punishment, the cruel old man was doomed to roam the world forever, guided only by a lamp constructed from a carved turnip and one coal from Hell. When Irish immigrants came to America, they were awestruck by the local pumpkin's size and carving possibilities.

The turnip was rapidly replaced by the plump orange harvest produce, and the carved-out snaggle-toothed Halloween jack-o'lantern was formed.

The vegetable most associated with Halloween...the jack-o'-lantern, which has its origins in British tradition as well. Jack was a folktale trickster who outraged not just God but also the devil with his many pranks and sins.

He was refused entry into both heaven and hell upon his death, but the devil unwillingly flung him a lump of burning coal, which Jack captured in a hollowed turnip and which would light his night walk on the hearth until Judgment Day...

The Oxford English Dictionary dates the term "jack-with-the-lantern" to 1663, and "Jack of lanthorns" to 1704, both referring to a night watchman...by 1817, the jack-o-lantern is definitely connected with terrifying pranks—but not explicitly with Halloween or hollowed turnips.

Although every contemporary chronicle of the festival claims that vegetable lanterns were a time-honored component of Halloween festivities in the British Isles, none provides any source evidence. In reality, carved lanterns are not mentioned at all in any of the main nineteenth-century chroniclers of British festivals and folk traditions. ...

The Oxford English Dictionary has no indication of when the Halloween connection started; it acknowledges the United States as the major source of the present meaning of the jack-o'lantern, followed by England and Ireland, but no dates or sources are provided.

Apples

Apples and nuts were thought to be effective predictors in medieval England. For ages, Celtic communities employed them in their Halloween divination games, and certain Scottish, Irish, and British men and women—people from the northern portions of England—celebrated All Hallows with apples and nuts...

The night of October 31 was known as "Snap Apple Night" in areas of the British Isles...the term arose from an ancient game in which the player's wrists were tied behind his back and he tried to eat an apple strung from a string...

Americans, like their English forefathers, utilized apple dunking to choose who would marry first. Whoever could pluck an apple from a large pail of water with their hands tied behind their back would be married the quickest.

The Romans imported their pagan myths and celebrations to Britain, such as the harvest festival of Pomona, goddess of the orchards, on November 1 and the masked revels of Saturnalia, the winter solstice. Pomona's connection to the apple undoubtedly contributed to the fruit's eventual significance in Halloween games and celebrations.

Cake

People often offered cake gifts to deities to ward off their bad influence. They also gave a cake to the souls of the deceased, thinking that it would sustain them on their long trip to the otherworld. Soul cakes, baked on October 28th in honor of All Souls' Day, are one of the most well-known instances of pastries for the deceased.

Many pagan peoples, including the early Celts, thought that today was the day the dead awoke and roamed about on the earth and that unless they were nourished, the spirits would attack the living. Soul cakes are dark in certain parts of Germany, implying death. Cakes were laid on graves by the Ainu people of Germany and Austria, and they were put into tombs by the ancient Egyptians.

People in Europe provided soul cakes to the deceased to sustain them on their trip to the otherworld, or used cakes as offerings during funerals and feasts. It became customary to eat cakes on All Souls' Day. In Belgium, people thought that for every cake devoured on this day, one soul was liberated from purgatory.

Nuts

Since Roman times, nuts have been utilized for magic. Some inhabitants in Scotland and northern England thought nuts were so potent sorcerers that they named their

October 31st festival "Nut Crack Night"... Chestnuts and walnuts, both abundant during the harvest season, were favored in early divination games.

The most famous game is as follows: two nuts are named, one for each possible lover, and placed on a grate in the fire. She who is curious about the future observes and waits. If a nut burns true and steady, it means the lover will be loyal; if it pops in the heat, it means the guy cannot be trusted.

Kale

Young people in Scotland walked blindfolded into the garden to pluck kale stalks; afterward, in front of the crackling fireplace, the plants were "read" for showing signals of the future bride or husband—short and stunted, tall and healthy, withered and elderly, and so on.

The quantity of dirt sticking to the root was thought to represent the amount of dowry or riches a player may anticipate from a spouse. The stalks were then strung in a row above the entrance, and each successive Halloween guest was allocated a vegetable spouse in turn. Cabbage and leeks were utilized in the same way.

TRICK-OR-TREAT

The origin and symbolism

The old Catholic soul-sale custom was replaced by the custom of begging for food from house to house on Halloween. Originally charitable, "souling" evolved into a popular term over time.

Irish Halloween begging was usually accompanied by a disguise... but who performed the begging and what they were pursuing varied by location. A mummers' parade honored All Hallows Eve in Ireland's

County Cork... Those who provided food, wine, or money to the revelers were promised prosperity... This ritual of going from house to home in a masquerade and begging for food or money was done in America on Guy Fawkes Day, and for a few years even on Thanksgiving. The Irish Halloween masquerade became so popular that it influenced twentieth-century American trick-or-treating.

The development in America

"Trick or treating became widespread between 1920 and 1950, most likely beginning in the richer sections of the East and gradually expanding to rural areas of the West and South." Reports of trick-or-treaters date back to the late 1920s in Wellesley, Massachusetts, but not until the 1940s in North Carolina, Florida, and Texas. By the 1950s, every American youngster had heard of the ritual... Trick or treating on Halloween dates back centuries.

Guy Fawkes Day was an early American precursor. The holiday, which was popular in the east throughout the 17th and 18th centuries, faded out in most localities around the time of the American Revolution. Thanksgiving, on the other hand, was being observed regularly at the time, and it became a Thanksgiving tradition for youngsters to dress up and beg from house to house on the final Thursday in November.

Initially, the impoverished children would dress in rags and ask their richer neighbors for "something for Thanksgiving." Soon, all types of youngsters were engaged, and the habit expanded in popularity, as did the costumes. The Thanksgiving masquerade remained as late as the 1930s, then faded, and Halloween costumes and parades started to acquire national popularity...As for begging, the idea of accepting candy presents on Halloween owed much to the preceding decades' public gatherings."

Sometime in the middle of the 1930s, fed up with soaped windows and worse, ambitious housewives started experimenting with a home-based variant on the traditional protection racket established between retailers and Thanksgiving ragamuffins.

The American Home piece is noteworthy because it seems to be the first time the phrase "trick or treat" appears in a mass-circulation monthly in the United States... Trick-or-treating most likely originated in the plethora of planned events conducted by schools and civic organizations around the nation particularly to combat vandalism.

The postwar years are often considered the golden age of trick-or-treating. Halloween, like the consumer economy, has grown by leaps and bounds. Major candy businesses such as Curtiss and Brach, no longer bound by sugar restrictions, launched nationwide Halloween advertising campaigns. Previously a limited, hit-or-miss event, trick-or-treating was now a nationwide responsibility.

Generation 'Baby Boomers'

We Boomer kids have fond memories of Halloween Trick-or-Treating. Most of us also collected money, usually pennies, for Unicef in milk carton-shaped cardboard containers distributed at school. It was a neighborhood event, and our biggest fear was cold, rainy nights when mom insisted on us wearing coats over our costumes. Every neighborhood had at least one house that did not take part. That was all part of the legend.

The after-party ritual was just as enjoyable as the candy gathering itself. We threw our "loot" on the kitchen table to count, sort, and plan our meals. Mom or Dad sifted through our chocolates, removing any pieces they thought were dirty. They also welcomed "donations" of unwanted stuff. Until approximately junior high, most of us trick-or-treated. When your neighbors said, "Aren't you a bit old for this?" you realized it was time to call it quits. Then, with a smirk, they stuffed whatever was left into our bags and turned out the porch light.

CANDY FOR HALLOWEEN

Halloween candy from the early 1900s

"Halloween candies." Every ounce tastes as amazing as it looks! I create these sweets in our pristine candy kitchen, and I know what I'm talking about when I say they're pure, healthful, and wonderful to eat. Today's specials include: Nut Kisses—Mexican, vanilla, and strawberry, lb...25 cents; Buttercups—all flavors, nut and cream centers, lb...25 cents; Meadowbrook Caramels—our famous full cream caramels, vanilla, vanilla English walnut, vanilla filbert, maple...lb...25 cents; Waldorf Chocolates and Bonbon or all Chocolates, lb...25 cents; Halloween

Halloween treats from the 1920s

There was a profusion, almost a chaos, of orange and black sweets." There were orange gumdrops, jelly beans, buttercups, chips, and hard candies. And there were black (licorice) gumdrops, jelly beans, buttons, and every other gadget ever seen in black candy.

There were gorgeous and delicate opera sticks in both orange and black, frequently laced with ribbon and for the center of some of the never-ending arrangements of these things in Halloween candy boxes—witch and black cat ornaments on them—and eventually tied with magnificent pompoms of black...ribbon.

1950s Halloween confections

Brach's Harvest Jelly Beans, Brach's Harvest Panned Mix, Hershey's Kisses, Hershey's Miniatures, Goelitz Candy Corn Fleers Double Bubble Gum, Pure Sugar Apples, Jordan Almonds, Goetze's Caramel Creams, Reed's Butterscotch Squares, Midgee Tootsie Rolls, Starlight Kisses, Roasted Peanuts in Shell, Tootsie Roll Handi Pak, Chocolate Bridge Mixture, Spiced Jelly Drops, Chocolate Nonpareils, and Fireside Marshmallows

1960s Halloween confections

Never before, it seemed to us, have the food shops been supplied with such a wide variety and unique packets of sweets, cookies, chewing gum, and other goods meant to supply you with an easy bounty for those young trick-or-treaters who will soon be making their Halloween excursions." A comprehensive list would take up more room than I have. However, two novelties piqued our interest. One is a cellophane bag containing 14 small Sun-Maid Raisin cartons. Although I believe they will appeal to children, they are also suitable as snacks for adults at any time of year.

The second item is a new TV Time Popcorn box that includes a distinctive plastic 'feed bag'—similar to an apron with a large pocket across the front—that can be worn around a child's neck.

The feed bag is designed to contain fistfuls of popcorn, but it may also be used by any youngster on trick-or-treat rounds to collect other goodies. Aside from the feedbag, the TV Time Popcorn carton contains two packs of corn grains, oil, and salt, each with enough for three quarts of popcorn.

Candies

Ruth, Baby
Bubble gum with a bazooka
Gum beechnut
Bit-O-Honey\sButterfingers
Cigarettes with Candy
Sweet Corn
Kisses of Candy
Caramels
Peppermints in Chocolate
Chuckles
Chunky\sCracker Face suckers Jack Cutie (lollipops)
Fruit Drops Forever Yours
Hershey's Milk Chocolate Almond Bars
Fins Huck
Beans in a Jar
Mints for Juniors
M&M's Life Savers...
almond, peanut, and plain
M&M Chocolate M&M Wafer Bar Fruit Snacks
Mason Candy

Milky Way Mint Juleps (chewy) Wafer "money bags"
Nestle Milk Chocolate and Almond Nestle Bars
Henry Bars!
Pal chewing gum
Kisses with peanut butter
Popsicle Polly (fruit flavor)
Balls of popcorn
Powerful bars
Snickers
Three Musketeers
Rolls of taffy
Popsicle Tootsie Rolls
Miniatures of Tootsie Rolls
Whoppers
Wrigley's chewing gum

What role does candy corn play?

The first mentions of candy corn (also known as chicken feed) credit Goelitz (now the Jelly Belly firm) with introducing the dessert to the American public. There is no relation to Halloween or the autumn season. A decade earlier, professional confectionery recipes for exotic Indian Corn developed.

There is undoubtedly a link between corn and autumn and the harvest season. Around Halloween, several individuals adorned their homes with cornstalks. Our examination of past American newspapers indicates that candy corn was significant to many people, although it was not always associated with Halloween. I discovered advertisements published throughout the year. As an example:

Holiday Sales...

25 cents for a pound of Goelitz Candy Corn in a cello bag. Three-color buttercream confection fashioned like a genuine corn kernel. It's something to brag about."

"It is claimed that chatting about the good old days is a clear indicator of becoming older." Maybe I'm already returning to my second childhood since I had a sudden need for chicken-feed corn and jelly beans the other day and couldn't find them at my corner shop...

Confectionery corn, like many other Halloween delicacies, was pushed as a Halloween treat by candy corporations following WWII. Candy corn may have been particularly popular since it was a seasonal (autumn) treat. Other seasonal (autumn) sweets that are often converted to Halloween include popcorn balls and candied apples. Here are some other thoughts.

Corn from India

Many novel things were created by professional confectioners in the late nineteenth century. These things were made available by advancements in candy-producing equipment and methods.

This inventive delicacy may have inspired candy corn (also known as chicken scratch).

[1883]

Indian Corn Imitation

The following is a pretty excellent imitation of actual Indian corn: Boil the sugar in the usual manner and with the usual amount of cream of tartar; flavor and color the boil yellow; pull half of it and case it over with the plain sugar; loosen the screws in a pair of thumb rollers a little and pass the boil through; cut the pieces about the length of the corn pod, and when cold fold them over loosely in shape.

Menus for historic Halloween parties

[1901] Halloween Party: While the dictionary meaning of Halloween differs from the present young boy's understanding, say with all sincerity, give

the boys a nice time now and then, and why not on Halloween?

Boys will be far less likely to carry off the clothes posts, unhinge the gates, and make the night hideous if you give them a part in keeping with the occasion—a party where tin horns from the first course at the dinner table—where colored paper, napkins, folded to represent the "jack-be-nimble" and "jack-be-quicks," "toads," "monkeys," and "parrots,"

[1905]
Halloween Box Cake: The newest trend in Halloween supper-table décor is a cake constructed of white pasteboard boxes shaped like pie slices that slot together to provide the illusion of a huge cake. Each package is wrapped in white paper that looks like icing. At the end of the feast, the pieces are dispersed, each box carrying a little Halloween souvenir. Of course, one box holds a ring, another a thimble, a third a

silver piece, a fourth a mitten, a fifth a fool's hat, and so on. As the boxes are opened, much fun is had, and the individual who obtains the ring is joyfully applauded. The unfortunate person who receives the fool's hat must wear it for the rest of the evening.

Halloween Bash

On Halloween, all formalities must be abandoned. Not only will quaint traditions and mythological tricks be in order, but the décor and refreshments, as well as the meeting location, must be as weird and mysterious as possible. A spacious barn is unquestionably the ideal kind of accommodation for a rural or suburban house.

If this is not possible, a large attic running the length of the house is the next best option; however, if this is also denied to the ambitious hostess, let the kitchen be the place of meeting and mystery, with the dining-room, cleared of its usual furniture and decorated suitably for the occasion, reserved for the refreshments. Only Jack-o'-lanterns hung around the kitchen and candles in the dining room should provide lighting.

No matter how large the room, the decorations do not have to be expensive to be charming.

Large vases of ferns and chrysanthemums and umbrella stands of fluffy grasses would be ideal, but if they are unavailable, plenty of gayly tinged fall leaves will suffice. Festoons of nuts, bunches of wheat or oats, and strings of cranberries may also assist to enliven the wall decorations, and the nuts and cranberries can be used to decorate the refreshment table in a variety of unusual ways.

Make the table long enough (even if it means extending the length of the barn or loft) to accommodate all of the visitors at once. Arrange enormous platters of gingerbread in each corner, with dishes of simple sweets and nuts here and there, and fruit pyramids that will be swiftly devoured as the visitors gather around the table. There will be no formal waiting.

Suggestions for Halloween: Browning nuts, popping corn, cooking apples, and toasting marshmallows can greatly to the enjoyment of the evening. The dining table should be wrapped in pale green crepe paper, with lovely orange lights above.

Pumpkins of varied sizes should be scooped and scraped to form a hollow shell and set in the center of the table, lined with wax paper and loaded with tasty treats. Lighted candles and quaint oriental lanterns will add greatly to the decorations.

[1911] *Halloween Spreads*

Menu No. I: Ganser Salad, Brown Bread Sandwiches, Raised Loaf Cake, Priscilla Popped Corn, Hot Coffee.

Menu No. II: Rob's Rarebit, Zephyrettes, Sultana Fudge, German Punch

Menu No. III: Hamlin Ham Timbales, Ribbon Sandwiches, Nut Ginger Cookies, Penuche, Cider"

[1914] "Never were Halloween Decorations so Gay as This Year—Some Delicious Candy Recipes for the Festival. Each year there are so many new decorations for Halloween and so many good old ones revived that the only shame is that Halloween doesn't last for a week. And surely never before were there such attractive Halloween decorations as there is this year...

For a centerpiece on the table on which the refreshments are placed at a children's Halloween party are set forth, nothing is more interesting than a huge paper pumpkin, with green leaves and a greed stem. After the pumpkin and leaves are made, they can be varnished to make them stiff.

A little doll, dressed in yellow crepe paper, is seated on the top of the pumpkin and it is drawn by half a dozen little gray mice that can be bought at any toy or favorite store.

Each piece has a piece of yellow ribbon tied about its neck, with the other end in the hand of the doll Cinderella... Another Halloween idea that is good is a big Japanese paper parasol covered with yellow crepe paper, with two eyes, a nose, and a mouth cut out of black paper, and touched up with white paint.

These are fastened on the outside of the parasol, the nose over the tip, and the effect is delightful. Small gummed seals that can be used for decorative purposes come cut out and sold in packages. There are owls and witches, pumpkins, imps, and cats. An effective but easily made place card is a small white card with a seal pasted in one corner or at one end.

[1927] "The Halloween Lunch: Meat Sandwiches, Dill Pickles, Doughnuts, Sweet Cider, Pumpkin Pie, Raw Apples, Nuts."

[1932] "Halloween Parties: The colors of Harvest time make Halloween party decorations the gayest of all the year. Color and the mystery of benevolent witchcraft are a great help to the gayety of such a party and should set the pace. One of the most successful decorations for a Halloween party I ever used was a large copper tray loaded with fruit. The tray was oval. In the center was a small pumpkin surrounded by apples, oranges, pears, and clusters of green and purple grapes. The grapes trailed gracefully over the sides.

A decoration of this sort arranged on a table or sideboard and flanked by 8 or 10 candles of orange color suggests the opulence of harvest. Candlelight is so appropriate for Halloween it is a good idea to have the rooms lighted entirely this way with orange candles on sticks everywhere. Another attractive lighting arrangement is orange-colored paper lanterns. Paint Jack O'Lantern faces on the lanterns with black India Ink.

A large pumpkin with eyes, nose, and mouth cut out and a burning candle should occupy a prominent place in the room. Of course, witches, black cats, and skeletons should be purchased and hung about the room. Successful table decoration is made from oranges. Cut the tops from the oranges, and scoop out the pulp with a teaspoon. Cut Jack O'Lantern's faces in them. Place a tiny candle holder and candle in the lanterns.

The holders and tapers used for birthday cakes are excellent. Marigolds or orange and yellow button chrysanthemums are the flowers to use for the supper table. Sprays of orange Japanese Lantern flowers are beautiful and just the color for a Halloween party. Now for the menus. There is as much orange in the men as possible, so that the Halloween color scheme may be carried out.

Menu No. 1 Glorified Club Sandwiches, Spiced Pears, Olives. Mince or Pumpkin Pie, Coffee, Sugared Nuts, Halloween Candies

Menu No. 2 Shrimp Wiggle, Celery Curls, Mixed Sweet Pickles, Orange Cream in Orange Baskets< Assorted Frosted Cakes, Coffee, Nuts and Cluster Raisins, Halloween Candies

Menu No. 3 Chicken or Oyster Patties, Sweet Pickled Gherkins, Cranberry Jelly, Ice Cream, Halloween Orange Cake, Salted Almonds, Candied Ginger, Candies, Coffee

Menu No. 4 Chicken Bouillon with Whipped Cream, Cheese Crackers, Crab Salad, Hot Buttered Rolls, Dill Pickles, Orange Sherbet, Assorted Frosted Cakes, Candy, Coffee, Nuts.

A Ghostly Halloween Party

Everyone, whether he is fourteen or ninety, enjoys a ghost party. The invitations could be decorated with a skull and crossbones and tell guests to dress in ghostly attire. Make the room dark, and as guests enter, they should be greeted with a ghostly handclasp; a wet glove filled with sand works well.

A witch's cauldron (made from a cooking pot) bubbles on the hearth, stirred by a crone who sings the incantation from Macbeth as she tosses in toy snakes, frogs, and so on. She also tells fortunes for those who are interested.

A black paper cloth with white ghosts pasted on it can be used to cover the budget supper table for a ghost party. The focal point could be a witch's cauldron (a black pot with a grinning face chalked on one side) filled with tiny dangling ghosts made from pipe cleaners that serve as favors. The only light comes from white tapers stuck in black bottles.

Hot Ham Shortcakes with Cheese Sauce, Dill Pickle Sticks, Celery Curls, Radishes, Pumpkin-face Tarts, Ice-cold Coca-Cola, Chicken Corn (candy), Nuts, Apples on a Stick."

[1937] "Halloween Suppers Halloween Salad Cream Cheese Sandwiches Nuts, Apples, Taffy Orange-filled CupCakes Sweet Cider"

Meat Pies with Goblin Faces (faced slashed in the crust)

Carrot Julienne, Orange Ice in Orange Cups, Chocolate Cookies, Ginger Ale

[1942] Halloween Party: Make Halloween invitations out of black cats, cauldrons, scarecrows, pumpkins, or witches cutouts. Use black or orange paper and write the invitation as a jingle or as a simple note. Room decorations are a simple matter because they can be as informal as you want.

Spread a few sheaves of corn around the room, or place some stalks of corn among a riot of gay autumn leaves.

To provide light, use orange or black candles or orange bulbs—just a few to create an eerie effect. Large cutouts of black cats, witches, or pumpkins pinned to the walls around the room, as well as brilliant orange, yellow, or red tablecloths made of cotton or old sheets dyed in any of those colors, add to the party's theme.

Playing games based on the theme of the occasion, such as pulling fortunes from the witches' cauldron or spirit rapping, are popular at this type of party. Don't forget that traditional cider and doughnuts, orange and black candies, ice cream molds with a pumpkin, or made-with-honey pumpkin pie all contribute significantly in terms of decoration.

[1949]
Witches and hobgoblins have arrived in town, ready to attend children's Halloween parties." Never before have stores been so well stocked with orange and black paper masks, favors, and other festive decorations. Bakeries sell ginger-cookie owls and frosted cakes on which an elderly lady rides her broom. She can also be found in some candy stores molded in milk chocolate and, most amazing of all, modeled in ice cream. Halloween means carving pumpkins with eyes, ears, and noses and lighting a candle in the hollowed center... In the eyes of

children, "homemade" surprises are just as magical as store-bought ones.

They'll be overjoyed to discover a marshmallow face floating in their hot chocolate. Two melted chocolate or frosting dots squeezed through a pastry tube from the eyes, one on the nose, and one on the mouth. Alternatively, using a pastry tube, draw a whiskered cat's face on an orange-frosted cake. Make popcorn balls and decorate them with crepe paper hats and frosting faces.

[1952]
Halloween parties are an old, old custom that I particularly enjoy observing. Children and adults alike enjoy the spirit of giving on this old fateful night, so let's plan a Halloween party today. The merrymakers will enjoy refreshments that emphasize the eerie atmosphere of old traditions. Witches Candle Cakes with mint chocolate wafers are sure to please whether served with ice

cream, fruit, or hot cocoa... Popcorn and apples should also make an appearance at a Halloween party.

(2) Pigs in Blankets, Carrot Straws, Ripe Olives, Orange Sherbet, Chocolate Cupcakes with Orange Butter Icing (Jack O'Lantern faces traced on icing with melted chocolate).

[1957]
For the small fry, Halloween night is a crucial knight. Whether you're throwing a large-scale party or simply entertaining the visiting ghosts, a table of clever edibles with appropriate decorations will make you a popular hostess.

The eerie atmosphere can be easily and cheaply created with impish orange candles. Draw faces on brightly colored oranges with a crayon, soft pencil, or black enamel... Halloween Candy Apples are another hit with the pigtail crowd... Of course, Halloween parties are not just for kids. It's the ideal time to kick off the fall entertaining season.

[1963]
No other time of year provides a better opportunity for the colorful decorations that children adore. Make use of Halloween-themed paper plates and napkins.

Fill small paper cups with assorted Halloween candy and place one at each location. Allow your child to assist in the creation of the invitations, which should be orange jack-o-lanterns or round black cats cut out of construction paper. Make costumes a requirement. Give out prizes to the best.

Sloppy Joes and Halloween Cake (Chocolate Cake with Fudge Frosting, Decorated with Candy Corn, Ice Cream, and Hot Cocoa) are on the menu.

[1964] Halloween Party: Bob for apples, pumpkin carving, spooky games...

Witches' Cauldron Soup, Goblin Franks, Vegetable Relishes, Ice Cream Jack-O-Lanterns, and Milk Halloween Cookies are on the menu.

Dia de los Muertos (Day of the Dead) [Mexico]

Historians generally agree that modern Day of the Dead celebrations are Christianized versions of pagan celebrations from the past. There appear to be some conflicting reports as to which holiday was morphed.

The Aztecs recognized two death gods.

The darker of the two was Mictecacihuatl. His birthday was traditionally celebrated in the ninth month (August in our calendar).

The other god was kinder and gentler, and his celebration was closer to today's dates.
The Ancient Aztecs' View on Death

To the Aztecs, cosmic balance and this life would be impossible unless sacrificial blood was offered to forces of life and fertility such as the sun, rain, and earth. In Aztec myth, the gods sacrificed themselves so that the newly created sun could move on its path. .. The accounts written in Spanish and Nahuatl in the sixteenth century provide detailed descriptions of Aztec concepts of death and the afterlife. .. People who died of illness or old age were taken to Mictlan, the dark underworld ruled by the skeletal god of death, Mictlantecuhtli, and his consort, Mictlancihuatl.

The corpse was dressed in paper vestments, wrapped and tied in a cloth bundle, and cremated, along with a dog to serve as a guide through the underworld, in preparation for this journey. The road to

Mictlan wound through a dangerous landscape... Mictlan was a place with no exits and no way out.

Aside from the dreary...realm of Mictlan, there was Tlalocan's afterworld, the paradise of Tlaloc, the god of rain and water. This was a place of eternal spring, abundance, and wealth for those who died by lightning, drowning, or were afflicted by a specific disease... These people, who were related to Tlaloc, were buried whole, rather than cremated, with images of the mountain gods...

The Aztecs held yearly ceremonies for the dead over two consecutive twenty-day months, the first for children and the second for adults, with a special emphasis on the cult of warrior souls. Although these ceremonies took place in the late summer of August, many aspects of them have been carried over into the fall Catholic celebrations of All Saints' Day and All Souls'

Day. Marigolds, a flower specifically associated with the dead in the Aztec ritual, frequently play a major role in contemporary celebrations, along with the ritual offering of food for the visiting dead.

Death celebrations in ancient Aztec culture

These [Ancient Aztec] people, like the rest, observed the ninth month of the year of twenty days on the eighth month of August by our calendar. The festival held at the beginning of this month was joyfully celebrated.

It was known as Micialhuitontli, which means "Feast of the Little Dead." According to my information, the diminutive was used to commemorate the deaths of innocent children. Offerings and sacrifices were made to honor and venerate these children during the solemn ceremonies of this day.

The second reason for naming this feast the diminutive is the same as for the previous feast. That is, it was a preparation for the upcoming festival, known as the Great Feast of the Dead when adults were to be remembered. Another reason (and the main one) was based on omens and superstition.

Because this feast fell on August 8th, these people were concerned about crop loss due to frost at the beginning of August. Thus, the natives prepared their offerings, oblations, and sacrifices for this and the following month's feasts.

As I previously stated, the first reason for the name Feast of the Little Dead stemmed from the offerings made for deceased children. I'd like to mention something that happened to me on Allhallows Day and the Day of the Faithful Departed.

When I inquired as to why offerings were made on Allhallows, I was told that it was in honor of the children, as it was an ancient custom that had survived. When I asked if offerings were made on the Day of the Faithful Departed, I was told that they were, but only in honor of adults. I was saddened to hear these things because I could see that the Feast of the Little Dead and [the feast] of the Adults was still being observed.

On the first day, I saw people selling chocolate, candles, fowl, fruit, large amounts of seed, and food. The next day, I saw the same thing being done. Though this feast occurred in August, I suspect that if it is an evil simulation (which I cannot confirm), the pagan festival has been moved to the Feast of Allhallows to conceal the ancient ceremony...

This main festival lasted the entire month, until the start of the Great Feast of the Dead. On this day, the largest thick tree trunk the woods could produce was cut down. The bark was removed and smoothed. Once completed, it was brought and placed at the city or town's entrance. When it arrived, the priests emerged from the temples, carrying trumpets and singing and dancing. "Common men appeared with conch shells, offerings, food, copal incense burners, and other types of incense."

The Catholic Church Relationship

Early Spanish observers...remarked on the fabrication of idols from edible grains and their distribution as talismans or articles of communion...pre-Columbian practices were simply annexed to the All Souls' festival; sometimes with the approval of Franciscan friars who wished to encourage the rapid conversion of the indigenous population to Christianity...

Father Diego de Duran, writing in 1580, was troubled by the way indigenous cults of the dead were transposed to All Saints and All

Souls'. He was especially concerned that All Saints' had become a festival devoted to deceased small children, emulating the pre-Christian feast of Miccailhuitontli...which had traditionally occurred two months earlier.

Scholars in Mexico disagree about the impact of these ancient festivals on the popular practice of Todos Santos...as the Day of the Dead is sometimes referred to.

However, an overemphasis on the pre-Columbian past can easily obscure the fact that there are striking similarities between the Day of the Dead rituals and the early modern observance of All Souls' Day in Europe. Yellow mourning flowers were common in both sixteenth-century Spain and Mexico... In the old Castilian province of Zamora, funeral rites included ofrendas and banquets. Food stands in Barcelona routinely sold seasonal sweets known as panellets del morts, or All Saints Day.

Other cakes and sweets were also popular during the holidays in Catalonia, Sardinia, Portugal, the Azores, and Haute-Saone in France, just as soul cakes were in pre-Reformation Britain.

The widespread consumption of anthropomorphic foods, or foods shaped like humans, appears to be unique to the Mexican Todos Santos. Sugared skulls and human-shaped figurines were among them. These included the sugared skulls and figurines that have gained international attention, as well as the pan de Muertos, "bread figures in the style of angels and humans," which took on a "ritual character."

Bread in human or animal form, in particular, was made throughout the Iberian peninsula, though rarely for this holiday. There are reasons to believe that the Mexican Day of the Dead was a complex mix of Mesoamerican and European influences, rather than a holiday onto which Christian observances were imposed. In this regard, the Day of the Dead was not dissimilar to Halloween.

Both had a shared European heritage as well as a dynamic fusion of pre-Christian and Christian beliefs. If this is the case, their differences may be rooted not only in the peculiarities of that syncretism but also in how the two holidays evolved in the New Worlds.

Contemporary observance

In Mexico, the Dia de Los Muertos festival embodies the best of both popular Catholicism and national cuisine." People build altars in their homes and graveyards across the country to feed the souls of the dead. Church officials observe two holy days in memory of the faithful departed: November 1 (All Saints' Day) and November 2 (All Souls' Day). According to popular belief, the angelitos (deceased children) return on the evening of October 31, and the adults the next night, though dates in local celebrations range from October 28 to November 4.

The feast of the dead began as ancestor worship, and the clergy was initially hesitant to incorporate such pagan practices into the liturgical calendar. Because it coincided with the maize harvest, the festival had particularly strong associations with pre-Hispanic agrarian cults. The cleaning of the graves and the construction of the altar kick off the celebrations.

At home, this consists of a table or platform hung from the ceiling, covered in a white cloth, and supporting a palm frond arch. Flowers, particularly cempasuchil (marigold), the 'flower of the dead,' adorn the ofrenda... Bread, water, and salt are always included in the foods offered to the dead, regardless of age or taste.

The bread is made with a special egg dough that is shaped into bones and a skull in the center. Sugar candies resembling skulls and Calaveras (skeletons) are also popular. Bakers in Oaxaca and Michoacán shape bread to resemble humans or animals. Children's offerings are small and straightforward: bread, candies, fruits, and milk or soft drinks.

The adult dead are given the finest foods, including adult bread and sugar figures, candied pumpkin, and other sweets. Mole (turkey in a rich chili sauce) and tamales are more elaborate preparations (corn dumplings stuffed with meat and chili and steamed in husks or banana leaves). Soft drinks, coffee, chocolate, beer, or tequila are all popular beverages among the spirits… The Day of the Dead has recently become a popular tourist attraction in towns like Mixquic, near Mexico City, and in the state of Oaxaca.

Recipe and food notes

Pan de Muerto (literally, the bread of the dead) is popular all over the world. Sugar skulls are also available. Other foods are determined by what the person liked when he or she was alive. Here are some observations:

Mexico celebrates El Dia de Los Muertos every year (Day of the Dead). The holiday begins on the evening of October 31 and lasts all day on November 2. It is a time when Mexican families remember their ancestors by fusing ancient beliefs and rituals of Mexico's early peoples with customs introduced by the Spanish Christians.

Much planning goes into the holiday, which is a pleasant commemoration rather than a solemn occasion, as one might expect. It is a very social event that begins with cleaning the gravesite and decorating it with flowers, as well as preparing special foods for their departed, such as pan de Muertos (bread of the dead). Family members gather at the cemetery to picnic and tell stories about the deceased.

In our day, the Day of the Dead is celebrated with catholic-pagan ceremonies throughout the country, but particularly in the states of Puebla, Mexico, Oaxaca, and Michoacan...people, in happy contrast to the sad day, place offerings of sweets, fruits, and tasty dishes of all kinds to their dead relatives...

Figures and pictures placed on a kind of altar represent the Christian part. The pagan portion is set up on a table or sideboard beneath the altar, which is draped in a beautifully embroidered tablecloth... Because this ceramic ware is only used at this time, the dishes, jobs, and pans are made of black glazed clay, as if for a special rite.

The glazed dishes are filled with turkey mole, pork or chicken, a dessert made of pumpkin, choke-cherries, and guavas; toasted sesame seed is sprinkled over the dishes; a dessert called punche, which is a kind of pudding of ground maize of different colors, blue, purple, and red; fruits of the season oranges, limes, choke-cherries, jicamas, and others; skulls made of sugar with the eye sockets stuffed with Tamales and the deceased's favorite foods...are also included among the offerings...

Both the ritual and the offerings appear to be similar to those of Aztec ceremonies held in Teotleco, the twelfth month of the Aztec calendar.

Teotelco was nearing the end of the year when we left in October. The priests washed the feet of the god Tlamatizicatl Titlacauan or Tezcatlipoca on the eighteenth day, and it was a joyful day.

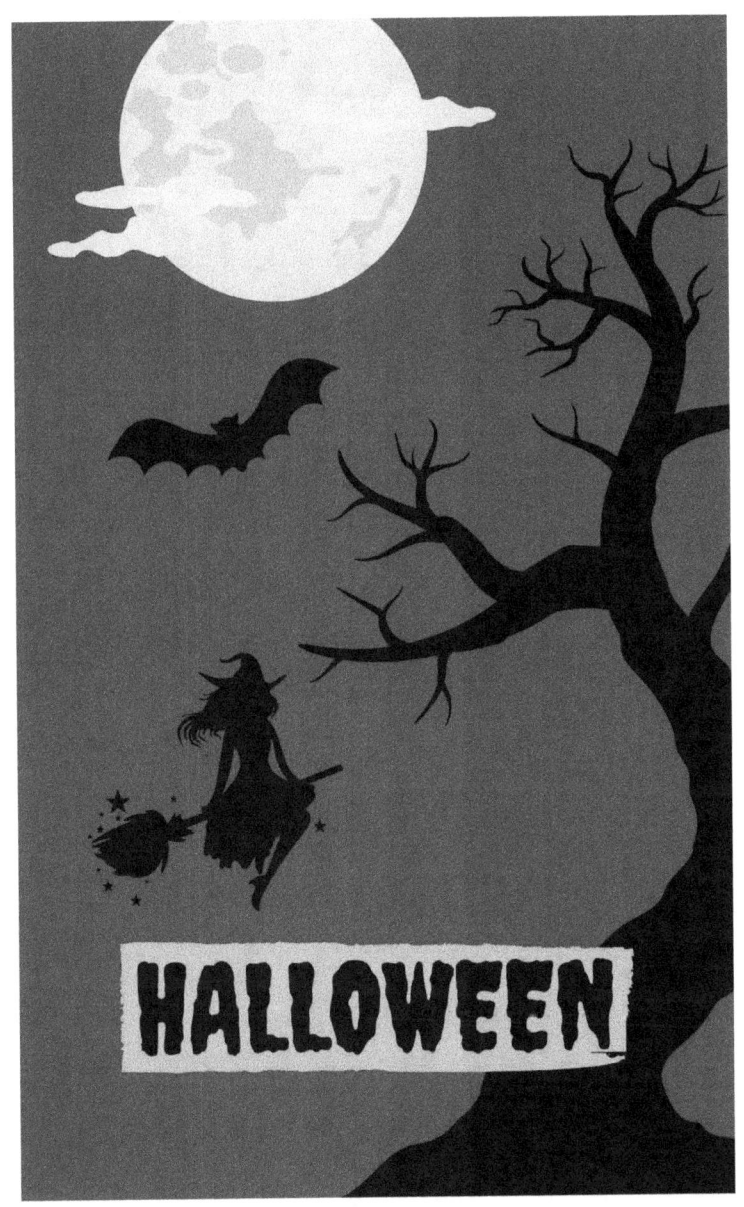

www.ingramcontent.com/pod-product-compliance
Lightning Source LLC
Chambersburg PA
CBHW070245220526

45465CB00004B/1534